Ten Po[ems]
about Sw[imming]

Candlestick Press

Published by:

Candlestick Press,
Diversity House, 72 Nottingham Road, Arnold, Nottingham NG5 6LF
www.candlestickpress.co.uk

Design and typesetting by Craig Twigg

Printed by Ratcliff & Roper Print Group, Nottinghamshire, UK

Selection and Introduction © Samantha Wynne-Rhydderch, 2022

Cover illustration © Sara Boccaccini Meadows, 2022
www.boccaccinimeadows.com

Candlestick Press monogram © Barbara Shaw, 2008

© Candlestick Press, 2022

Donation to Surfers Against Sewage
www.sas.org.uk

ISBN 978 1 913627 06 5

Acknowledgements

The poems in this pamphlet are reprinted from the following books, all by
permission of the publishers listed unless stated otherwise. Every effort has been
made to trace the copyright holders of the poems published in this book. The
editor and publisher apologise if any material has been included without
permission or without the appropriate acknowledgement, and would be glad to be
told of anyone who has not been consulted.

Thanks are due to all the copyright holders cited below for their kind permission:

Vievee Francis, *Forest Primeval: Poems* (Evanston: TriQuarterly Books/
Northwestern University Press, 2016). Copyright © 2016 by Vievee Francis.
Published 2016 by TriQuarterly Books/Northwestern University Press. All rights
reserved. Paul Henry, first published in this anthology by kind permission of the
author https://paulhenrypoet.co.uk. Ranjit Hoskote, *Atlas of Lost Beliefs*
(Arc Press, 2019). Hannah Lowe, *Chick* (Bloodaxe Books, 2013)
www.bloodaxebooks.com. Katrina Naomi, *Same But Different* by Katrina Naomi
& Helen Mort (Hazel Press, 2021). The poem won the 2021 Keats-Shelley Poetry
Prize and was published here by kind permission of the author. Nicholas Murray,
Acapulco (Melos Press, 2012). Jay Parini, *New and Collected Poems: 1975-2015*
(Beacon Press, 2017). Katherine Pierpoint, *Truffle Beds* (Faber & Faber, 1995).
Stevie Smith, *Collected Poems and Drawings of Stevie Smith*, ed. Will May
(Faber & Faber, 2018); *All the Poems* (New Directions, 2016), copyright
© 1937, 1938, 1942, 1950, 1957, 1962, 1966, 1971, 1972. Copyright © 2016 by
the Estate of James MacGibbon. Copyright © 2015 by Will May. Samantha
Wynne-Rhydderch, poem first published in this anthology, by kind permission of
the author.

All permissions cleared courtesy of Suzanne Fairless-Aitken
c/o Swift Permissions swiftpermissions@gmail.com

Where poets are no longer living, their dates are given.

Introduction

Sea, swimming pool or river: the places where we swim are also places of encounter, be that with other swimmers, seals, seaweed or with a new understanding of ourselves. Entering the water can be a moment of transition, releasing us from gravity to a place of levity which allows space for reflection, offering a new perspective on the dry land we've temporarily left behind.

Hannah Lowe's poem encapsulates two kinds of reflection: the humorous ("legs of men") and the mysterious ("the pool spread like a sunken ballroom"). The swimming pool is the place where many of us learn to swim, so I was thrilled to be able to include Katherine Pierpoint's exquisite account of learning to swim, not in a pool but rather on a piano stool. Stevie Smith's classic poem propels us from childhood to adulthood on the turn of a verb (to wave), reminding us how the gesture of waving can, like the sea, shift suddenly in meaning from 'fun' to 'help'. Vievee Francis's poem 'Black River' expands on the idea of water as a place of transition where we can enter into a new state; and this is precisely the experience of the speaker of Katrina Naomi's prizewinning poem about swimming underwater through kelp, in which we explore a world that is near, yet so unfamiliar "it's like any place almost visited".

As we dive further into the anthology we are invited to accompany the speakers in their encounters with animals and fish, whether Nicholas Murray's seal or Ranjit Hoskote's protagonist who develops scales and gills. Jay Parini's 'Swimming after Thoughts' returns us to a space of reflection, as does Paul Henry's delicate cameo of a swimmer captured in stained glass.

For those of us with disabilities, swimming may no longer – or ever – have been an option: my own poem explores the impact of developing Ménières Disease on my relationship to water. My hope is that this collection will appeal both to armchair swimmers as well as to those who have yet to dip a toe in the water.

Samantha Wynne-Rhydderch

What I Think About When I'm Swimming

Legs.
>The thick, muscular legs of men
>>I do not know.
>The water is my friend. It holds us all.
Is it beautiful
>to watch me swim? Like the paddlewheel
>>of an old steam boat I go.
The time I couldn't swim, sunlight blanking out
>the children's faces where I surfaced,
flailing in a riot of rubber rings and screams.
>Now I cannot drown,
>>I keep the steady course,
I only hear the water babble in my ear,
>the fizz of bubbles from the man in front
who sprints with the ego of a fish,
>>new to these parts.
>It is boring to watch me swim.
What is beautiful are the tiles
>with their century of rust,
>>the pool spread like a sunken ballroom,
marbled with the winter sun and here,
>the deep end's edge
where I hang breathless,
>wet and warm and sad
>>and the warehouse roofs rise up
beyond the glass,
>like a painting of another land.

Hannah Lowe

Swim Right Up to Me

I first learnt to swim at home in my father's study
On the piano-stool, planted on the middle of the rug.
Stomach down, head up, arms and legs rowing hard;
I swam bravely, ploughing up the small room,
Pinned on a crushed stuckness of stomach to tapestry,
The twin handles hard on my elbows on the back-stroke.
A view down through four braced wooden legs
To the same thin spot in the rug.
My mother faced me, calling rhythmic encouragement,
Almost stepping back to let me swim up to her,
Reminding me to breathe;
And wiping my hair and eyes with her hand
As I swam and swam on the furniture against a running tide,
Pig-cheeked, concentrating on pushing and pushing away,
Planning to learn to fly next, easy,
Higher than the kitchen table, even. The garden wall.

Katherine Pierpoint

Not Waving but Drowning

Nobody heard him, the dead man,
But still he lay moaning:
I was much further out than you thought
And not waving but drowning.

Poor chap, he always loved larking
And now he's dead
It must have been too cold for him his heart gave way,
They said.

Oh, no no no, it was too cold always
(Still the dead one lay moaning)
I was much too far out all my life
And not waving but drowning.

Stevie Smith (1902 – 1971)

Black River

She thought to throw herself in, to
take to the water what had been released,
unraveled, swirled about her like hair
in high wind, like the current in spring,
season of beginnings, she thinks, as she tucks up
her cotton dress, the white one.

That she had held something like that
within for so long was a wonder to her,
though she was no simple woman (despite
her bare feet and their indiscretion).
She had a mind to become someone acceptable,
a woman who did not draw on her arms,
a woman who did not jump as a girl would,
so many ways to disappoint, to wear down
the surrounding world. She means to surrender
to the rippling. Why not? The water
bracing in the cold melt.

Now that she no longer carried what had held her
for so long, nor cared who knew, she says to no one
in particular, *Let the river carry me like a shell*
to unknown waters, let me be filled with another
spirit, this time, one that will see and abide.

Vievee Francis

in the kelp forest

the first time she finds herself   among brown strands
between fear and wonder   floating   in this other world   of
upside down   a place a person could wed herself to   so much
dank silence   beyond her breath   the gentle murmur of
limbs   in suspension   their arc and splay   there's no
peace like this in the dry country   she's like a body in a jar at
the lab   but keeps her Dutch colours   sliding her mind
through slender lengths of weed   fabric-like   plastic-like
part translucent   part shine   like nothing else but kelp   her
restless hair goes on its own pulsing journey   she forgets
for blissed moments   she can't breathe here   this isn't air
waves nudge overhead   it's like any place almost visited
say a city   say Seville   and she talks half-seriously   half
what-if   of how she might live here   the kelp wafts in
welcome   displays its tentacles   as she refuses neoprene
longs for kelp's beckon   and touch   longs to pass as a local
a strange fish for sure   but one who could belong

Katrina Naomi

The Swimming Pool

You're dripping away, shedding water and scales
as you climb

out of the pool, giddy, gills wilting into lungs:
searing balloons

of trapped oxygen. The light and lyrical self
is burning up on re-entry.

Purged, it stumbles from a wet pelt
sloughed off on the floor.

*

Shavings of sky, sawn by the wind, drop on the water.
You flick away the light of unreported moons.

Never disturb dust, attachments or silences.
The handprint you left on the wall
when you came out of the pool
is drying in the noon-heat:

you're a thumb and a digit
away from extinction.

*

Noon-shards: a grey man's hacking at a block of ice
with a sickle. Leaves shimmer on the water

that flinches like the skin of a sleeping dog
when he trawls the tree-fall with a frayed net.

Your body is a gathering intensity of shadows
broken by a surge of glass.

Regent of vacancy, gather up the folded bathrobe
from the abandoned chair. Settle

under the deck umbrella
whose shadow has migrated across the pool.

*

He gives in by degrees
to the slurp and sluice.
Little deaths claim his time.

Now another he enters his mind, tissues, cells:
that he is plunging through the upside-down sky
to catch the diver's farewell, the lost pearl.

*Centaur foundling, surviving twin: they wrote me
on the brittlest pages of the songbook.
I'm wearing this season for the last time:
for the last time this green shawl, these leaves twisted*

to form a diadem. Next year he will return
as fire, gulls floating above his head.
His image will trail behind him
in a canal of shouts and whispers.

Thank you, he will say to the lifeguard,
That is not my skull you have there

in the raven's mask.

Ranjit Hoskote

Swimming

Climbing the stairs for example. How is that like swimming?
With an attack of Ménières my arms are out in front as if swimming

to stop myself falling. When the bureau and the fridge start to float
down the hall and the stair rail is a rope thrown, I'm swimming

in a disease that goes away and comes back like the tide.
But in its own time. It surprised me so often I had to stop sea swimming.

And there's no cure, I remember as the contents of my stomach
bloom across the hall walls where the furniture is on its back swimming.

Are you drunk? someone calls. The house isn't flooded but my body is
diluted by a disease that requires a firm eye on an horizon that's swimming.

Often it seems I'm being rescued by the house which itself turns
into a boat rocked in the storm in which I'm still swimming.

With Ménières people can no longer drive or swim or we'll drown.
All I have is the memory of stepping into the sea's pink silk, then swimming.

On July evenings I would swim towards the setting sun along a line of light
strung off the end of the quay, joining dots that spelled this is me swimming.

How can I forget the evening the stars slung a net over the sky, and the sun slid
into the sea like a coin in slow motion – my last memory of swimming?

Samantha Wynne-Rhydderch

Island Swimmer

She is too quick for me:
only a ripple as arms
slice through the calmed,
cooled sea, late afternoon.

Her deft, aquatic grace
reminds us of our clumsy,
walrus-like advance
towards the shore.

Her ancient skin
like supple leather
glistens in last light;
effortless, she emulates

the action of the eel,
that wriggles in the depths
beneath a white caique
which rocks beside the quay.

Nicholas Murray

Swimming after Thoughts

In memoriam: Robert Penn Warren

Across the blackened pond and back again,
he's swimming in an ether all his own;

lap after lap, he finds the groove
no champion of motion would approve,

since time and distance hardly cross his mind
except as something someone else might find

of interest. He swims and turns, making
his way through frogspawn, lily pads, and
shaking

reeds, a slow and lofty lolling stroke
that cunningly preserves what's left to stoke

his engines further, like a steamwheel plunging
through its loop of light. He knows that lunging

only breaks the arc of his full reach.
He pulls the long, slow oar of speech,

addressing camber-backed and copper fish;
the minnows darken like ungathered wishes,

flash and fade – ideas in a haze of hopes
ungathered into syntax, sounding tropes.

The waterbugs pluck circles round his ears
while, overhead, a black hawk veers

to reappraise his slithering neck and frogs
take sides on what or who he is: a log

or lanky, milk-white beast. He goes on swimming,
trolling in the green-dark glistening

silence and subtending mud where things
begin, where thoughts amass in broken rings

and surface, break to light, the brokered sound
of lost beginnings – fished for, found.

Jay Parini

The Swimmer in the Glass

after 'Boneless Blue' – a stained glass panel by Angharad Whitfield

A pane slips its cloud's frame,
is stained by a thousand summers.
Half-woman, half-glass swims in it.

And the sun stares into her
and she stares back between strokes
at the shifting galleries of sky.

And the hills stare into her,
a hawk's cross, a lost sheep
and the stray, midday moon.

And she stares back as she lies
catching the lake's breath,
sustained by the fathomless blue.

Paul Henry